The Bible Study
MAP
A Creative Journal

BARBOUR BOOKS
An Imprint of Barbour Publishing, Inc.

Published by Barbour Books, an imprint of Barbour Publishing, Inc., 1810 Barbour Drive, Uhrichsville, Ohio 44683, www.barbourbooks.com

Our mission is to inspire the world with the life-changing message of the Bible.

Member of the
Evangelical Christian
Publishers Association

Printed in China.

What Does Daily Bible Study Look Like? . . .

Get ready to dig deep into God's Word with this creative journal. . .where every colorful page will guide you to create your very own Bible study map—as you write out specific thoughts, ideas, and questions, which you can follow (from start to finish!)—as you begin your journey into the scriptures. (Be sure to record the date on each one of your Bible study maps so you can look back over time and see how God's Word has been reflected in your daily life!)

The Bible Study Map will not only encourage you to spend time focusing on and thinking about the life-changing truths of God's Word. . .it will also help you build a healthy spiritual habit of daily Bible study for life!

Don't know where to begin? Check out the helpful list of recommended Bible study topics at the back of this book!

DATE:

Bible study topic:

....

My scripture reading for today:

....

....

....

My response to this passage of scripture:

....

....

....

....

....

....

....

....

....

....

....

What this means to my faith:

....

....

....

....

....

....

....

....

....

....

....

....

....

....

....

....

How it applies to my daily life:

....

....

....

Other thoughts on
this topic:

....

....

....

....

....

....

....

....

....

....

....

Questions I have for digging
deeper into scripture:

....

....

....

....

....

My prayer for today:

....

....

....

....

....

....

*All Scripture is breathed out by God and profitable
for teaching, for reproof, for correction, and for
training in righteousness, that the man of God may
be complete, equipped for every good work.*

2 TIMOTHY 3:16–17

DATE:

Bible study topic:

....

My scripture reading for today:

....

....

....

What this means to my faith:

....

....

....

....

....

....

....

....

....

....

My response to this passage of scripture:

....

....

....

....

....

....

....

....

....

....

....

....

....

....

....

....

....

....

....

....

How it applies to my daily life:

....

....

....

Other thoughts on this topic:

....

....

....

....

....

....

....

....

....

....

....

Questions I have for digging deeper into scripture:

....

....

....

....

....

My prayer for today:

....

....

....

....

....

....

"This Book of the Law shall not depart from your mouth, but you shall meditate on it day and night, so that you may be careful to do according to all that is written in it."

JOSHUA 1:8

DATE:

Bible study topic:

....

My scripture reading for today:

....

....

....

What this means to my faith:

....

....

....

....

....

....

....

My response to this passage of scripture:

....

....

....

....

....

....

....

....

....

....

....

....

....

....

....

....

....

....

How it applies to my daily life:

....

....

....

Other thoughts on
this topic:

....

....

....

....

....

....

....

....

....

....

....

....

Questions I have for digging
deeper into scripture:

....

....

....

....

....

My prayer for today:

....

....

....

....

....

....

*Your word is a lamp to my feet
and a light to my path.*
PSALM 119:105

Bible study topic:

....

My scripture reading
for today:

....

....

....

What this means
to my faith:

....

....

....

....

....

....

....

My response to this
passage of scripture:

....

....

....

....

....

....

....

....

....

....

....

....

....

....

....

....

....

....

....

....

....

....

How it applies to my daily life:

....

....

....

Other thoughts on this topic:

....

....

....

....

....

....

....

....

....

....

....

....

Questions I have for digging deeper into scripture:

....

....

....

....

....

My prayer for today:

....

....

....

....

....

....

Do not forget my teaching, but let your heart keep my commandments, for length of days and years of life and peace they will add to you.

PROVERBS 3:1-2

DATE:

Bible study topic:

....

My scripture reading
for today:

....

....

....

My response to this
passage of scripture:

....

....

....

....

....

....

....

....

....

....

....

What this means
to my faith:

....

....

....

....

....

....

....

....

....

....

....

....

....

....

....

....

....

....

....

How it applies to my daily life:

....

....

....

Other thoughts on this topic:	Questions I have for digging deeper into scripture:

Other thoughts on this topic:

....

....

....

....

....

....

....

....

....

....

....

....

Questions I have for digging deeper into scripture:

....

....

....

....

....

My prayer for today:

....

....

....

....

....

....

*Open my eyes, that I may behold
wondrous things out of your law.*
PSALM 119:18

DATE:

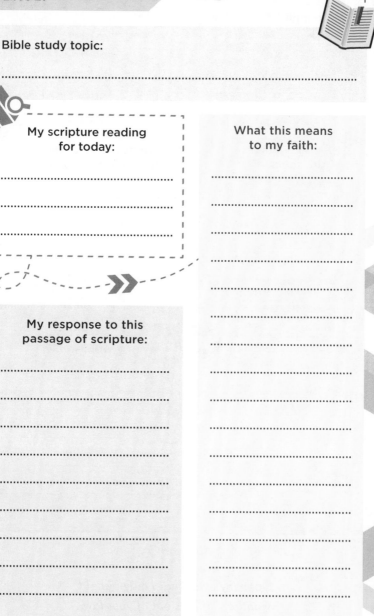

Bible study topic:

....

My scripture reading for today:

....

....

....

What this means to my faith:

....

....

....

....

....

....

....

....

....

....

....

....

....

....

My response to this passage of scripture:

....

....

....

....

....

....

....

....

....

....

How it applies to my daily life:

....

....

....

Other thoughts on this topic:

....

....

....

....

....

....

....

....

....

....

....

....

Questions I have for digging deeper into scripture:

....

....

....

....

....

My prayer for today:

....

....

....

....

....

....

For the word of God is living and active, sharper than any two-edged sword, piercing to the division of soul and of spirit, of joints and of marrow, and discerning the thoughts and intentions of the heart.

HEBREWS 4:12

DATE:

Bible study topic:

....

My scripture reading
for today:

....

....

....

What this means
to my faith:

....

....

....

....

....

....

....

My response to this
passage of scripture:

....

....

....

....

....

....

....

....

....

....

....

....

....

....

....

....

....

....

....

....

....

How it applies to my daily life:

....

....

....

Other thoughts on
this topic:

....

....

....

....

....

....

....

....

....

....

....

....

Questions I have for digging
deeper into scripture:

....

....

....

....

....

My prayer for today:

....

....

....

....

....

....

*"We live by every word that comes
from the mouth of the LORD."*
DEUTERONOMY 8:3 NLT

DATE:

Bible study topic:

....

My scripture reading
for today:

....

....

....

What this means
to my faith:

....

....

....

....

....

....

....

My response to this
passage of scripture:

....

....

....

....

....

....

....

....

....

....

....

....

....

....

....

....

....

....

....

....

....

....

....

How it applies to my daily life:

....

....

....

Other thoughts on this topic:

....

....

....

....

....

....

....

....

....

....

....

....

Questions I have for digging deeper into scripture:

....

....

....

....

....

My prayer for today:

....

....

....

....

....

....

But be doers of the word, and not hearers only, deceiving yourselves.
JAMES 1:22

DATE:

Bible study topic:

....

My scripture reading
for today:

....

....

....

What this means
to my faith:

....

....

....

....

....

....

....

My response to this
passage of scripture:

....

....

....

....

....

....

....

....

....

....

....

....

....

....

....

....

....

....

....

....

....

....

How it applies to my daily life:

....

....

....

Other thoughts on
this topic:

....

....

....

....

....

....

....

....

....

....

....

....

Questions I have for digging
deeper into scripture:

....

....

....

....

....

My prayer for today:

....

....

....

....

....

....

*Wise words are more valuable
than much gold and many rubies.*
PROVERBS 20:15 NLT

DATE:

Bible study topic:

....

My scripture reading for today:

....

....

....

What this means to my faith:

....

....

....

....

....

....

....

....

....

....

....

....

....

....

....

My response to this passage of scripture:

....

....

....

....

....

....

....

....

....

....

....

How it applies to my daily life:

....

....

....

Other thoughts on this topic:

....

....

....

....

....

....

....

....

....

....

....

Questions I have for digging deeper into scripture:

....

....

....

....

....

My prayer for today:

....

....

....

....

....

....

*If you look carefully into the perfect law that sets you free,
and if you do what it says and don't forget what you
heard, then God will bless you for doing it.*

JAMES 1:24-25 NLT

Bible study topic:

....

My scripture reading
for today:

....

....

....

My response to this
passage of scripture:

....

....

....

....

....

....

....

....

....

....

....

What this means
to my faith:

....

....

....

....

....

....

....

....

....

....

....

....

....

....

....

....

....

How it applies to my daily life:

....

....

....

Other thoughts on
this topic:

....

....

....

....

....

....

....

....

....

....

....

....

Questions I have for digging
deeper into scripture:

....

....

....

....

....

My prayer for today:

....

....

....

....

....

....

*So we must listen very carefully to the truth we
have heard, or we may drift away from it.*
HEBREWS 2:1 NLT

DATE:

Bible study topic:

....

My scripture reading for today:

....

....

....

What this means to my faith:

....

....

....

....

....

....

....

....

....

My response to this passage of scripture:

....

....

....

....

....

....

....

....

....

....

....

....

....

....

....

....

....

....

....

How it applies to my daily life:

....

....

....

Other thoughts on
this topic:

....

....

....

....

....

....

....

....

....

....

....

Questions I have for digging
deeper into scripture:

....

....

....

....

....

My prayer for today:

....

....

....

....

....

....

*"And you will know the truth,
and the truth will set you free."*
JOHN 8:32

DATE:

Bible study topic:

....

My scripture reading
for today:

....

....

....

My response to this
passage of scripture:

....

....

....

....

....

....

....

....

....

....

....

What this means
to my faith:

....

....

....

....

....

....

....

....

....

....

....

....

....

....

....

....

....

....

How it applies to my daily life:

....

....

....

Other thoughts on
this topic:

....

....

....

....

....

....

....

....

....

....

....

Questions I have for digging
deeper into scripture:

....

....

....

....

....

My prayer for today:

....

....

....

....

....

....

*If you receive my words and treasure up my commandments
with you. . .yes, if you call out for insight and raise your
voice for understanding, if you seek it like silver. . .
then you will understand the fear of the
LORD and find the knowledge of God.*

PROVERBS 2:1-5

Bible study topic:

....

My scripture reading
for today:

....

....

....

What this means
to my faith:

....

....

....

....

....

....

....

My response to this
passage of scripture:

....

....

....

....

....

....

....

....

....

....

....

....

....

....

....

....

....

....

How it applies to my daily life:

....

....

....

Other thoughts on this topic:

....

....

....

....

....

....

....

....

....

....

....

Questions I have for digging deeper into scripture:

....

....

....

....

....

My prayer for today:

....

....

....

....

....

....

In the beginning was the Word, and the Word was with God, and the Word was God.

JOHN 1:1

Bible study topic:

....

My scripture reading
for today:

....

....

....

What this means
to my faith:

....

....

....

....

....

....

....

My response to this
passage of scripture:

....

....

....

....

....

....

....

....

....

....

....

....

....

....

....

....

....

....

How it applies to my daily life:

....

....

....

Other thoughts on
this topic:

....

....

....

....

....

....

....

....

....

....

....

Questions I have for digging
deeper into scripture:

....

....

....

....

....

My prayer for today:

....

....

....

....

....

....

*"The words that I have spoken
to you are spirit and life."*
JOHN 6:63

DATE:

Bible study topic:

....

My scripture reading for today:

....

....

....

My response to this passage of scripture:

....

....

....

....

....

....

....

....

....

....

What this means to my faith:

....

....

....

....

....

....

....

....

....

....

....

....

....

....

....

....

....

How it applies to my daily life:

....

....

....

Other thoughts on
this topic:

....

....

....

....

....

....

....

....

....

....

....

Questions I have for digging
deeper into scripture:

....

....

....

....

....

My prayer for today:

....

....

....

....

....

....

*So put away all malice and all deceit and hypocrisy and
envy and all slander. Like newborn infants, long for the pure
spiritual milk, that by it you may grow up into salvation.*
1 PETER 2:1-2

Bible study topic:

....

My scripture reading for today:

....

....

....

My response to this passage of scripture:

....

....

....

....

....

....

....

....

....

....

What this means to my faith:

....

....

....

....

....

....

....

....

....

....

....

....

....

....

....

....

....

How it applies to my daily life:

....

....

....

Other thoughts on this topic:

....

....

....

....

....

....

....

....

....

....

....

....

Questions I have for digging deeper into scripture:

....

....

....

....

....

My prayer for today:

....

....

....

....

....

....

But his delight is in the law of the LORD,
and on his law he meditates day and night.
PSALM 1:2

DATE:

Bible study topic:

....

My scripture reading
for today:

....

....

....

My response to this
passage of scripture:

....

....

....

....

....

....

....

....

....

....

What this means
to my faith:

....

....

....

....

....

....

....

....

....

....

....

....

....

....

....

....

How it applies to my daily life:

....

....

....

Other thoughts on
this topic:

....

....

....

....

....

....

....

....

....

....

....

....

Questions I have for digging
deeper into scripture:

....

....

....

....

....

My prayer for today:

....

....

....

....

....

....

*But grow in the grace and knowledge of our Lord
and Savior Jesus Christ. To him be the glory
both now and to the day of eternity. Amen.*

2 Peter 3:18

DATE:

Bible study topic:

....

My scripture reading for today:

....

....

....

What this means to my faith:

....

....

....

....

....

....

....

....

....

....

My response to this passage of scripture:

....

....

....

....

....

....

....

....

....

....

....

....

....

....

....

....

....

....

....

How it applies to my daily life:

....

....

....

Other thoughts on this topic:

....

....

....

....

....

....

....

....

....

....

....

....

Questions I have for digging deeper into scripture:

....

....

....

....

....

My prayer for today:

....

....

....

....

....

....

*Fix your thoughts on what is true, and honorable,
and right, and pure, and lovely, and admirable.
Think about things that are excellent
and worthy of praise.*

PHILIPPIANS 4:8 NLT

DATE:

Bible study topic:

....

My scripture reading
for today:

....

....

....

What this means
to my faith:

....

....

....

....

....

....

....

....

....

My response to this
passage of scripture:

....

....

....

....

....

....

....

....

....

....

....

....

....

....

....

....

....

....

....

How it applies to my daily life:

....

....

....

Other thoughts on this topic:

....

....

....

....

....

....

....

....

....

....

....

Questions I have for digging deeper into scripture:

....

....

....

....

....

My prayer for today:

....

....

....

....

....

....

May grace and peace be multiplied to you in the knowledge of God. . . . His divine power has granted to us all things that pertain to life and godliness, through the knowledge of him who called us to his own glory and excellence.

2 PETER 1:2–3

DATE:

Bible study topic:

....

My scripture reading for today:

....

....

....

What this means to my faith:

....

....

....

....

....

....

....

....

....

....

....

....

....

....

....

....

My response to this passage of scripture:

....

....

....

....

....

....

....

....

....

....

....

How it applies to my daily life:

....

....

....

Other thoughts on this topic:

....

....

....

....

....

....

....

....

....

....

....

....

Questions I have for digging deeper into scripture:

....

....

....

....

....

My prayer for today:

....

....

....

....

....

....

Let the word of Christ dwell in you richly,
teaching and admonishing one another in all wisdom,
singing psalms and hymns and spiritual songs,
with thankfulness in your hearts to God.

Colossians 3:16

DATE:

Bible study topic:

....

My scripture reading for today:

....

....

....

What this means to my faith:

....

....

....

....

....

....

....

....

My response to this passage of scripture:

....

....

....

....

....

....

....

....

....

....

....

....

....

....

....

....

....

....

....

....

How it applies to my daily life:

....

....

....

Other thoughts on this topic:	Questions I have for digging deeper into scripture:

Other thoughts on this topic:

....

....

....

....

....

....

....

....

....

....

....

Questions I have for digging deeper into scripture:

....

....

....

....

....

My prayer for today:

....

....

....

....

....

....

*If any of you lacks wisdom, let him ask God,
who gives generously to all without
reproach, and it will be given him.*

JAMES 1:5

DATE:

Bible study topic:

....

My scripture reading
for today:

....

....

....

My response to this
passage of scripture:

....

....

....

....

....

....

....

....

....

....

What this means
to my faith:

....

....

....

....

....

....

....

....

....

....

....

....

....

....

....

....

How it applies to my daily life:

....
....
....

Other thoughts on this topic:

....
....
....
....
....
....
....
....
....
....
....
....

Questions I have for digging deeper into scripture:

....
....
....
....
....

My prayer for today:

....
....
....
....
....
....

Blessed is the man who walks not in the counsel of the wicked, nor stands in the way of sinners, nor sits in the seat of scoffers; but his delight is in the law of the LORD, and on his law he meditates day and night.

PSALM 1:1-2

Bible study topic:

....

My scripture reading
for today:

....

....

....

What this means
to my faith:

....

....

....

....

....

....

My response to this
passage of scripture:

....

....

....

....

....

....

....

....

....

....

....

....

....

....

....

....

....

....

....

....

....

....

....

How it applies to my daily life:

....

....

....

Other thoughts on this topic:

....

....

....

....

....

....

....

....

....

....

....

....

Questions I have for digging deeper into scripture:

....

....

....

....

....

My prayer for today:

....

....

....

....

....

....

*Be a good worker, one who does not need
to be ashamed and who correctly
explains the word of truth.*
2 TIMOTHY 2:15 NLT

DATE:

Bible study topic:

....

My scripture reading
for today:

....
....
....

What this means
to my faith:

....
....
....
....
....
....
....
....
....
....
....
....
....
....
....
....

My response to this
passage of scripture:

....
....
....
....
....
....
....
....
....
....
....

How it applies to my daily life:

....

....

....

Other thoughts on this topic:

....

....

....

....

....

....

....

....

....

....

....

....

Questions I have for digging deeper into scripture:

....

....

....

....

....

My prayer for today:

....

....

....

....

....

....

*I will delight in your decrees
and not forget your word.*
PSALM 119:16 NLT

DATE:

Bible study topic:

....

My scripture reading
for today:

....

....

....

What this means
to my faith:

....

....

....

....

....

My response to this
passage of scripture:

....

....

....

....

....

....

....

....

....

....

....

....

....

....

....

....

....

....

....

How it applies to my daily life:

....

....

....

Other thoughts on
this topic:

....

....

....

....

....

....

....

....

....

....

....

....

Questions I have for digging
deeper into scripture:

....

....

....

....

....

My prayer for today:

....

....

....

....

....

....

*"So commit yourselves wholeheartedly to these words
of mine. Tie them to your hands and wear
them on your forehead as reminders."*
DEUTERONOMY 11:18 NLT

Bible study topic:

....

My scripture reading
for today:

....

....

....

What this means
to my faith:

....

....

....

....

....

....

....

My response to this
passage of scripture:

....

....

....

....

....

....

....

....

....

....

....

....

....

....

....

....

....

....

....

....

....

How it applies to my daily life:

....

....

....

Other thoughts on this topic:

....

....

....

....

....

....

....

....

....

....

....

....

Questions I have for digging deeper into scripture:

....

....

....

....

....

My prayer for today:

....

....

....

....

....

....

I have more understanding than all my teachers,
for your testimonies are my meditation.
PSALM 119:99

DATE:

Bible study topic:

....

My scripture reading
for today:

....

....

....

What this means
to my faith:

....

....

....

....

....

....

....

....

....

....

My response to this
passage of scripture:

....

....

....

....

....

....

....

....

....

....

....

....

....

....

....

....

....

....

....

How it applies to my daily life:

....

....

....

Other thoughts on
this topic:

....

....

....

....

....

....

....

....

....

....

....

....

Questions I have for digging
deeper into scripture:

....

....

....

....

....

My prayer for today:

....

....

....

....

....

....

*Never let loyalty and kindness leave you! Tie them around
your neck as a reminder. Write them deep within your
heart. Then you will find favor with both God and
people, and you will earn a good reputation.*

PROVERBS 3:3-4 NLT

Bible study topic:

....

My scripture reading
for today:

....

....

....

What this means
to my faith:

....

....

....

....

....

....

....

....

....

....

....

....

....

....

My response to this
passage of scripture:

....

....

....

....

....

....

....

....

....

....

How it applies to my daily life:

....

....

....

Other thoughts on this topic:

....

....

....

....

....

....

....

....

....

....

....

....

Questions I have for digging deeper into scripture:

....

....

....

....

....

My prayer for today:

....

....

....

....

....

....

He has granted to us his precious and very great promises, so that through them you may become partakers of the divine nature, having escaped from the corruption that is in the world because of sinful desire.

2 PETER 1:4

DATE:

Bible study topic:

....

My scripture reading
for today:

....

....

....

My response to this
passage of scripture:

....

....

....

....

....

....

....

....

....

....

What this means
to my faith:

....

....

....

....

....

....

....

....

....

....

....

....

....

....

....

....

....

How it applies to my daily life:

....

....

....

Other thoughts on this topic:

....

....

....

....

....

....

....

....

....

....

....

....

Questions I have for digging deeper into scripture:

....

....

....

....

....

My prayer for today:

....

....

....

....

....

....

And we know that for those who love God all things work together for good, for those who are called according to his purpose.
ROMANS 8:28

Bible study topic:

....

My scripture reading
for today:

....

....

....

My response to this
passage of scripture:

....

....

....

....

....

....

....

....

....

....

What this means
to my faith:

....

....

....

....

....

....

....

....

....

....

....

....

....

....

....

....

....

How it applies to my daily life:

....

....

....

Other thoughts on this topic:

....

....

....

....

....

....

....

....

....

....

....

....

Questions I have for digging deeper into scripture:

....

....

....

....

....

My prayer for today:

....

....

....

....

....

....

"For God so loved the world, that he gave his only Son, that whoever believes in him should not perish but have eternal life. For God did not send his Son into the world to condemn the world, but in order that the world might be saved through him."

JOHN 3:16–17

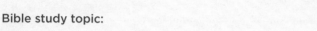

DATE:

Bible study topic:

....

My scripture reading
for today:

....

....

....

What this means
to my faith:

....

....

....

....

....

....

....

....

....

....

My response to this
passage of scripture:

....

....

....

....

....

....

....

....

....

....

....

....

....

....

How it applies to my daily life:

....

....

....

Other thoughts on this topic:

....

....

....

....

....

....

....

....

....

....

....

....

Questions I have for digging deeper into scripture:

....

....

....

....

....

My prayer for today:

....

....

....

....

....

....

You have been taught the holy Scriptures from childhood, and they have given you the wisdom to receive the salvation that comes by trusting in Christ Jesus.

2 Timothy 3:15 nlt

Bible study topic:

....

My scripture reading for today:

....

....

....

What this means to my faith:

....

....

....

....

....

....

....

My response to this passage of scripture:

....

....

....

....

....

....

....

....

....

....

....

....

....

....

....

....

....

....

....

....

....

....

How it applies to my daily life:

....

....

....

Other thoughts on this topic:

....

....

....

....

....

....

....

....

....

....

....

Questions I have for digging deeper into scripture:

....

....

....

....

....

My prayer for today:

....

....

....

....

....

....

For whatever was written in former days was written for our instruction, that through endurance and through the encouragement of the Scriptures we might have hope.

ROMANS 15:4

Bible study topic:

....

My scripture reading
for today:

....

....

....

What this means
to my faith:

....

....

....

....

....

....

....

My response to this
passage of scripture:

....

....

....

....

....

....

....

....

....

....

....

....

....

....

....

....

....

....

....

....

How it applies to my daily life:

....

....

....

**Other thoughts on
this topic:**

....

....

....

....

....

....

....

....

....

....

....

....

**Questions I have for digging
deeper into scripture:**

....

....

....

....

....

My prayer for today:

....

....

....

....

....

....

*How sweet are your words to my taste,
sweeter than honey to my mouth!*
PSALM 119:103

Bible study topic:

....

My scripture reading
for today:

....

....

....

What this means
to my faith:

....

....

....

....

....

....

....

My response to this
passage of scripture:

....

....

....

....

....

....

....

....

....

....

....

....

....

....

....

....

....

....

....

How it applies to my daily life:

....

....

....

Other thoughts on this topic:

....

....

....

....

....

....

....

....

....

....

....

....

Questions I have for digging deeper into scripture:

....

....

....

....

....

My prayer for today:

....

....

....

....

....

....

Don't worry about anything; instead, pray about everything. Tell God what you need, and thank him for all he has done. Then you will experience God's peace, which exceeds anything we can understand.

PHILIPPIANS 4:6-7 NLT

DATE:

Bible study topic:

....

My scripture reading for today:

....

....

....

What this means to my faith:

....

....

....

....

....

....

....

....

....

My response to this passage of scripture:

....

....

....

....

....

....

....

....

....

....

....

....

....

....

....

....

....

....

....

How it applies to my daily life:

....

....

....

Other thoughts on this topic:

....

....

....

....

....

....

....

....

....

....

....

....

Questions I have for digging deeper into scripture:

....

....

....

....

....

My prayer for today:

....

....

....

....

....

....

"Seek the Kingdom of God above all else, and live righteously, and he will give you everything you need."

MATTHEW 6:33 NLT

DATE:

Bible study topic:

....

My scripture reading
for today:

....

....

....

What this means
to my faith:

....

....

....

....

....

....

....

My response to this
passage of scripture:

....

....

....

....

....

....

....

....

....

....

....

....

....

....

....

....

....

....

....

....

How it applies to my daily life:

....

....

....

Other thoughts on this topic:

....

....

....

....

....

....

....

....

....

....

....

....

Questions I have for digging deeper into scripture:

....

....

....

....

....

My prayer for today:

....

....

....

....

....

....

Your words were found, and I ate them, and your words became to me a joy and the delight of my heart, for I am called by your name, O LORD, God of hosts.
JEREMIAH 15:16

Bible study topic:

....

**My scripture reading
for today:**

....

....

....

**What this means
to my faith:**

....

....

....

....

....

....

....

**My response to this
passage of scripture:**

....

....

....

....

....

....

....

....

....

....

....

....

....

....

....

....

....

....

....

....

....

....

How it applies to my daily life:

....

....

....

Other thoughts on this topic:

....

....

....

....

....

....

....

....

....

....

....

....

Questions I have for digging deeper into scripture:

....

....

....

....

....

My prayer for today:

....

....

....

....

....

....

" 'Man shall not live by bread alone, but by every word that comes from the mouth of God.' "

MATTHEW 4:4

DATE:

Bible study topic:

....

My scripture reading
for today:

....

....

....

My response to this
passage of scripture:

....

....

....

....

....

....

....

....

....

....

....

What this means
to my faith:

....

....

....

....

....

....

....

....

....

....

....

....

....

....

....

....

....

How it applies to my daily life:

....

....

....

Other thoughts on this topic:

....

....

....

....

....

....

....

....

....

....

....

....

Questions I have for digging deeper into scripture:

....

....

....

....

....

My prayer for today:

....

....

....

....

....

....

"Be careful to obey all these words that I command you, that it may go well with you and with your children after you forever, when you do what is good and right in the sight of the Lord your God."

DEUTERONOMY 12:28

Bible study topic:

....

My scripture reading
for today:

....

....

....

My response to this
passage of scripture:

....

....

....

....

....

....

....

....

....

....

....

....

What this means
to my faith:

....

....

....

....

....

....

....

....

....

....

....

....

....

....

....

....

....

....

How it applies to my daily life:

....

....

....

Other thoughts on this topic:

....

....

....

....

....

....

....

....

....

....

....

....

Questions I have for digging deeper into scripture:

....

....

....

....

....

My prayer for today:

....

....

....

....

....

....

"Come here and listen to the words of the LORD your God."
JOSHUA 3:9

Bible study topic:

....

My scripture reading
for today:

....

....

....

My response to this
passage of scripture:

....

....

....

....

....

....

....

....

....

....

....

What this means
to my faith:

....

....

....

....

....

....

....

....

....

....

....

....

....

....

....

....

How it applies to my daily life:

....
....
....

Other thoughts on this topic:

....
....
....
....
....
....
....
....
....
....
....
....

Questions I have for digging deeper into scripture:

....
....
....
....
....

My prayer for today:

....
....
....
....
....
....

"But even more blessed are all who hear the word of God and put it into practice."
Luke 11:28 NLT

Bible study topic:

....

My scripture reading
for today:

....

....

....

My response to this
passage of scripture:

....

....

....

....

....

....

....

....

....

....

What this means
to my faith:

....

....

....

....

....

....

....

....

....

....

....

....

....

....

....

....

How it applies to my daily life:

....

....

....

Other thoughts on
this topic:

....

....

....

....

....

....

....

....

....

....

....

....

Questions I have for digging
deeper into scripture:

....

....

....

....

....

My prayer for today:

....

....

....

....

....

....

Look to God's instructions and teachings!
Isaiah 8:20 NLT

DATE:

Bible study topic:

....

My scripture reading for today:

....

....

....

What this means to my faith:

....

....

....

....

....

....

....

....

....

....

....

....

....

....

....

....

....

....

....

....

My response to this passage of scripture:

....

....

....

....

....

....

....

....

....

....

....

How it applies to my daily life:

....

....

....

Other thoughts on this topic:

....

....

....

....

....

....

....

....

....

....

....

....

Questions I have for digging deeper into scripture:

....

....

....

....

....

My prayer for today:

....

....

....

....

....

....

*"The farmer plants seed by taking
God's word to others."*
MARK 4:14 NLT

Bible study topic:

....

My scripture reading
for today:

....

....

....

What this means
to my faith:

....

....

....

....

....

....

....

My response to this
passage of scripture:

....

....

....

....

....

....

....

....

....

....

....

....

....

....

....

....

....

....

....

....

How it applies to my daily life:

....

....

....

Other thoughts on this topic:

....

....

....

....

....

....

....

....

....

....

....

....

Questions I have for digging deeper into scripture:

....

....

....

....

....

My prayer for today:

....

....

....

....

....

....

*But those who obey God's word truly
show how completely they love him.
That is how we know we are living in him.*
1 JOHN 2:5 NLT

Bible study topic:

....

My scripture reading for today:

....

....

....

What this means to my faith:

....

....

....

....

....

....

....

My response to this passage of scripture:

....

....

....

....

....

....

....

....

....

....

....

How it applies to my daily life:

....

....

....

Other thoughts on this topic:

....

....

....

....

....

....

....

....

....

....

....

....

Questions I have for digging deeper into scripture:

....

....

....

....

....

My prayer for today:

....

....

....

....

....

....

For this is the love of God, that we keep his commandments. And his commandments are not burdensome.

1 John 5:3

DATE:

Bible study topic:

....

My scripture reading
for today:

....

....

....

What this means
to my faith:

....

....

....

....

....

....

....

....

My response to this
passage of scripture:

....

....

....

....

....

....

....

....

....

....

....

....

....

....

....

....

....

....

....

How it applies to my daily life:

....

....

....

Other thoughts on
this topic:

....

....

....

....

....

....

....

....

....

....

....

....

Questions I have for digging
deeper into scripture:

....

....

....

....

....

My prayer for today:

....

....

....

....

....

....

*Think over what I say, for the Lord will give
you understanding in everything.*
2 TIMOTHY 2:7

DATE:

Bible study topic:

....

My scripture reading
for today:

....

....

....

What this means
to my faith:

....

....

....

....

....

....

....

My response to this
passage of scripture:

....

....

....

....

....

....

....

....

....

....

....

....

....

....

....

....

....

....

....

....

....

How it applies to my daily life:

....

....

....

Other thoughts on this topic:

....

....

....

....

....

....

....

....

....

....

....

....

Questions I have for digging deeper into scripture:

....

....

....

....

....

My prayer for today:

....

....

....

....

....

....

For you have been born again, but not to a life that will quickly end. Your new life will last forever because it comes from the eternal, living word of God.

1 PETER 1:23 NLT

DATE:

Bible study topic:

....

My scripture reading for today:

....

....

....

My response to this passage of scripture:

....

....

....

....

....

....

....

....

....

....

What this means to my faith:

....

....

....

....

....

....

....

....

....

....

....

....

....

....

....

....

....

....

How it applies to my daily life:

....

....

....

Other thoughts on
this topic:

....

....

....

....

....

....

....

....

....

....

....

Questions I have for digging
deeper into scripture:

....

....

....

....

....

My prayer for today:

....

....

....

....

....

....

*So get rid of all the filth and evil in your lives, and humbly
accept the word God has planted in your hearts,
for it has the power to save your souls.*

JAMES 1:21 NLT

DATE:

Bible study topic:

....

My scripture reading
for today:

....

....

....

What this means
to my faith:

....

....

....

....

....

....

....

....

....

....

....

....

....

....

....

My response to this
passage of scripture:

....

....

....

....

....

....

....

....

....

....

....

....

....

....

How it applies to my daily life:

....

....

....

Other thoughts on this topic:

....

....

....

....

....

....

....

....

....

....

....

Questions I have for digging deeper into scripture:

....

....

....

....

....

My prayer for today:

....

....

....

....

....

....

"Pay attention to what you hear: with the measure you use, it will be measured to you, and still more will be added to you."

MARK 4:24

Bible study topic:

....

My scripture reading
for today:

....

....

....

What this means
to my faith:

....

....

....

....

....

....

My response to this
passage of scripture:

....

....

....

....

....

....

....

....

....

....

....

....

....

....

....

....

....

....

....

....

....

....

How it applies to my daily life:

....

....

....

Other thoughts on this topic:

....

....

....

....

....

....

....

....

....

....

Questions I have for digging deeper into scripture:

....

....

....

....

....

My prayer for today:

....

....

....

....

....

....

Remember your leaders who taught you the word of God. Think of all the good that has come from their lives, and follow the example of their faith.

HEBREWS 13:7 NLT

Bible study topic:

....

My scripture reading
for today:

....

....

....

My response to this
passage of scripture:

....

....

....

....

....

....

....

....

....

....

What this means
to my faith:

....

....

....

....

....

....

....

....

....

....

....

....

....

....

....

....

....

How it applies to my daily life:

....

....

....

Other thoughts on this topic:

....

....

....

....

....

....

....

....

....

....

....

....

Questions I have for digging deeper into scripture:

....

....

....

....

....

My prayer for today:

....

....

....

....

....

....

"I delight to do your will, O my God;
your law is within my heart."
PSALM 40:8

DATE:

Bible study topic:

....

My scripture reading
for today:

....

....

....

What this means
to my faith:

....

....

....

....

....

....

My response to this
passage of scripture:

....

....

....

....

....

....

....

....

....

....

....

....

....

....

....

....

....

....

....

....

How it applies to my daily life:

....

....

....

Other thoughts on this topic:

....

....

....

....

....

....

....

....

....

....

....

....

Questions I have for digging deeper into scripture:

....

....

....

....

....

My prayer for today:

....

....

....

....

....

....

The word of God cannot be chained.
2 TIMOTHY 2:9 NLT

Bible study topic:

....

My scripture reading for today:

....

....

....

What this means to my faith:

....

....

....

....

....

....

....

....

....

....

....

My response to this passage of scripture:

....

....

....

....

....

....

....

....

....

....

....

....

....

....

....

....

....

....

How it applies to my daily life:

....

....

....

Other thoughts on this topic:

....

....

....

....

....

....

....

....

....

....

....

....

Questions I have for digging deeper into scripture:

....

....

....

....

....

My prayer for today:

....

....

....

....

....

....

Since everything God created is good, we should not reject any of it but receive it with thanks. For we know it is made acceptable by the word of God and prayer.

1 TIMOTHY 4:4-5 NLT

Bible study topic:

....

My scripture reading for today:

....

....

....

My response to this passage of scripture:

....

....

....

....

....

....

....

....

....

....

....

What this means to my faith:

....

....

....

....

....

....

....

....

....

....

....

....

....

....

....

....

....

How it applies to my daily life:

....

....

....

Other thoughts on
this topic:

....

....

....

....

....

....

....

....

....

....

....

Questions I have for digging
deeper into scripture:

....

....

....

....

....

My prayer for today:

....

....

....

....

....

....

*And now the word of the Lord is ringing
out from you to people everywhere.*
1 THESSALONIANS 1:8 NLT

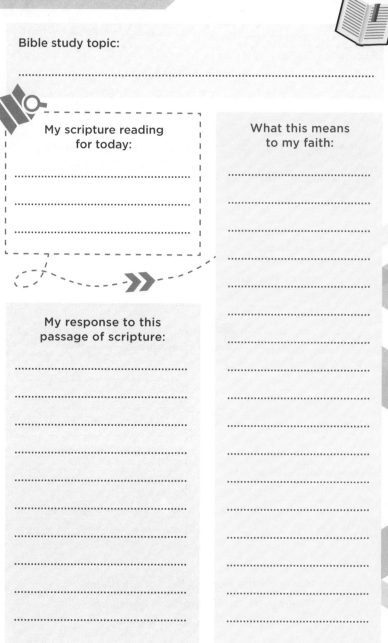

DATE:

Bible study topic:

....

My scripture reading
for today:

....

....

....

What this means
to my faith:

....

....

....

....

....

....

....

My response to this
passage of scripture:

....

....

....

....

....

....

....

....

....

....

How it applies to my daily life:

....

....

....

Other thoughts on this topic:

....

....

....

....

....

....

....

....

....

....

....

....

Questions I have for digging deeper into scripture:

....

....

....

....

....

My prayer for today:

....

....

....

....

....

....

This God—his way is perfect;
the word of the LORD proves true;
he is a shield for all those who take refuge in him.
PSALM 18:30

DATE:

Bible study topic:

....

My scripture reading
for today:

....

....

....

My response to this
passage of scripture:

....

....

....

....

....

....

....

....

....

....

What this means
to my faith:

....

....

....

....

....

....

....

....

....

....

....

....

....

....

....

....

....

How it applies to my daily life:

....

....

....

Other thoughts on this topic:

....

....

....

....

....

....

....

....

....

....

....

....

Questions I have for digging deeper into scripture:

....

....

....

....

....

My prayer for today:

....

....

....

....

....

....

We never stop thanking God that when you received his message from us, you didn't think of our words as mere human ideas. You accepted what we said as the very word of God. . . . And this word continues to work in you who believe.

1 THESSALONIANS 2:13 NLT

Bible study topic:

....

My scripture reading
for today:

....

....

....

What this means
to my faith:

....

....

....

....

....

....

....

....

....

....

....

....

....

My response to this
passage of scripture:

....

....

....

....

....

....

....

....

....

....

....

....

....

....

....

....

How it applies to my daily life:

....

....

....

Other thoughts on
this topic:

....

....

....

....

....

....

....

....

....

....

....

Questions I have for digging
deeper into scripture:

....

....

....

....

....

My prayer for today:

....

....

....

....

....

....

*Put on salvation as your helmet, and take the
sword of the Spirit, which is the word of God.*
EPHESIANS 6:17 NLT

Bible study topic:

....

My scripture reading for today:

....

....

....

My response to this passage of scripture:

....

....

....

....

....

....

....

....

....

....

....

What this means to my faith:

....

....

....

....

....

....

....

....

....

....

....

....

....

....

....

....

How it applies to my daily life:

....

....

....

Other thoughts on
this topic:

....

....

....

....

....

....

....

....

....

....

....

....

Questions I have for digging
deeper into scripture:

....

....

....

....

....

My prayer for today:

....

....

....

....

....

....

*We don't try to trick anyone or
distort the word of God.*
2 CORINTHIANS 4:2 NLT

DATE:

Bible study topic:

....

My scripture reading
for today:

....

....

....

My response to this
passage of scripture:

....

....

....

....

....

....

....

....

....

....

What this means
to my faith:

....

....

....

....

....

....

....

....

....

....

....

....

....

....

....

....

....

How it applies to my daily life:

....

....

....

Other thoughts on this topic:

....

....

....

....

....

....

....

....

....

....

....

....

Questions I have for digging deeper into scripture:

....

....

....

....

....

My prayer for today:

....

....

....

....

....

....

Trust in the LORD with all your heart,
and do not lean on your own understanding.
PROVERBS 3:5

DATE:

Bible study topic:

....

My scripture reading
for today:

....

....

....

My response to this
passage of scripture:

....

....

....

....

....

....

....

....

....

....

What this means
to my faith:

....

....

....

....

....

....

....

....

....

....

....

....

....

....

....

....

How it applies to my daily life:

....

....

....

Other thoughts on this topic:

....

....

....

....

....

....

....

....

....

....

....

....

Questions I have for digging deeper into scripture:

....

....

....

....

....

My prayer for today:

....

....

....

....

....

....

"Anyone who belongs to God listens gladly to the words of God."
JOHN 8:47 NLT

DATE:

Bible study topic:

....

My scripture reading for today:

....

....

....

What this means to my faith:

....

....

....

....

....

....

....

....

....

My response to this passage of scripture:

....

....

....

....

....

....

....

....

....

....

....

....

....

....

....

....

....

....

....

How it applies to my daily life:

....

....

....

Other thoughts on this topic:

....

....

....

....

....

....

....

....

....

....

....

....

Questions I have for digging deeper into scripture:

....

....

....

....

....

My prayer for today:

....

....

....

....

....

....

"For the word of God will never fail."
LUKE 1:37 NLT

DATE:

Bible study topic:

....

My scripture reading
for today:

....

....

....

What this means
to my faith:

....

....

....

....

....

....

....

....

....

My response to this
passage of scripture:

....

....

....

....

....

....

....

....

....

....

....

....

....

....

....

....

....

....

....

....

How it applies to my daily life:

....

....

....

Other thoughts on
this topic:

....

....

....

....

....

....

....

....

....

....

....

Questions I have for digging
deeper into scripture:

....

....

....

....

....

My prayer for today:

....

....

....

....

....

....

*The grass withers, the flower fades,
but the word of our God will stand forever.*
ISAIAH 40:8

Bible study topic:

....

My scripture reading
for today:

....

....

....

What this means
to my faith:

....

....

....

....

....

....

....

My response to this
passage of scripture:

....

....

....

....

....

....

....

....

....

....

....

....

....

....

....

....

....

....

....

....

....

How it applies to my daily life:

....

....

....

Other thoughts on this topic:

....

....

....

....

....

....

....

....

....

....

....

....

Questions I have for digging deeper into scripture:

....

....

....

....

....

My prayer for today:

....

....

....

....

....

....

"You search the Scriptures because you think they give you eternal life. But the Scriptures point to me!"
JOHN 5:39 NLT

Bible study topic:

....

My scripture reading
for today:

....

....

....

My response to this
passage of scripture:

....

....

....

....

....

....

....

....

....

....

What this means
to my faith:

....

....

....

....

....

....

....

....

....

....

....

....

....

....

....

....

....

....

....

How it applies to my daily life:

....

....

....

Other thoughts on this topic:

....

....

....

....

....

....

....

....

....

....

....

....

Questions I have for digging deeper into scripture:

....

....

....

....

....

My prayer for today:

....

....

....

....

....

....

God blesses the one who reads the words of this prophecy to the church, and he blesses all who listen to its message and obey what it says.

REVELATION 1:3 NLT

DATE:

Bible study topic:

....

My scripture reading
for today:

....

....

....

What this means
to my faith:

....

....

....

....

....

....

....

My response to this
passage of scripture:

....

....

....

....

....

....

....

....

....

....

....

....

....

....

....

....

....

....

....

....

How it applies to my daily life:

....

....

....

Other thoughts on this topic:

....

....

....

....

....

....

....

....

....

....

....

....

Questions I have for digging deeper into scripture:

....

....

....

....

....

My prayer for today:

....

....

....

....

....

....

Fear of the LORD is the foundation of true wisdom.
All who obey his commandments will grow
in wisdom. Praise him forever!
PSALM 111:10 NLT

DATE:

Bible study topic:

....

My scripture reading
for today:

....

....

....

My response to this
passage of scripture:

....

....

....

....

....

....

....

....

....

....

What this means
to my faith:

....

....

....

....

....

....

....

....

....

....

....

....

....

....

....

....

How it applies to my daily life:

....

....

....

Other thoughts on this topic:

....

....

....

....

....

....

....

....

....

....

....

....

Questions I have for digging deeper into scripture:

....

....

....

....

....

My prayer for today:

....

....

....

....

....

....

I'm asking GOD for one thing, only one thing:
to live with him in his house my whole life long.
I'll contemplate his beauty; I'll study at his feet.

PSALM 27:4 MSG

Bible study topic:

....

My scripture reading for today:

....

....

....

What this means to my faith:

....

....

....

....

....

....

....

....

....

....

....

....

....

....

....

My response to this passage of scripture:

....

....

....

....

....

....

....

....

....

....

How it applies to my daily life:

....

....

....

Other thoughts on
this topic:

....

....

....

....

....

....

....

....

....

....

....

....

Questions I have for digging
deeper into scripture:

....

....

....

....

....

My prayer for today:

....

....

....

....

....

....

*I find my delight in your
commandments, which I love.*
PSALM 119:47

Bible study topic:

....

My scripture reading
for today:

....

....

....

My response to this
passage of scripture:

....

....

....

....

....

....

....

....

....

....

What this means
to my faith:

....

....

....

....

....

....

....

....

....

....

....

....

....

....

....

....

How it applies to my daily life:

....

....

....

Other thoughts on this topic:

....

....

....

....

....

....

....

....

....

....

....

....

Questions I have for digging deeper into scripture:

....

....

....

....

....

My prayer for today:

....

....

....

....

....

....

Joyful is the person who finds wisdom, the one who gains understanding. For wisdom is more profitable than silver, and her wages are better than gold.

PROVERBS 3:13–14 NLT

DATE:

Bible study topic:

....

My scripture reading
for today:

....

....

....

What this means
to my faith:

....

....

....

....

....

....

....

....

....

....

....

....

....

....

....

....

....

My response to this
passage of scripture:

....

....

....

....

....

....

....

....

....

....

....

How it applies to my daily life:

....

....

....

Other thoughts on
this topic:

....

....

....

....

....

....

....

....

....

....

....

Questions I have for digging
deeper into scripture:

....

....

....

....

....

My prayer for today:

....

....

....

....

....

....

*"The Scripture you've just heard has
been fulfilled this very day!"*
LUKE 4:21 NLT

DATE:

Bible study topic:

....

My scripture reading
for today:

....

....

....

What this means
to my faith:

....

....

....

....

....

....

....

....

....

....

....

My response to this
passage of scripture:

....

....

....

....

....

....

....

....

....

....

....

....

....

....

....

....

....

....

....

How it applies to my daily life:

....

....

....

Other thoughts on this topic:

....

....

....

....

....

....

....

....

....

....

....

....

Questions I have for digging deeper into scripture:

....

....

....

....

....

My prayer for today:

....

....

....

....

....

....

"This is all happening to fulfill the words of the prophets as recorded in the Scriptures."
MATTHEW 26:56 NLT

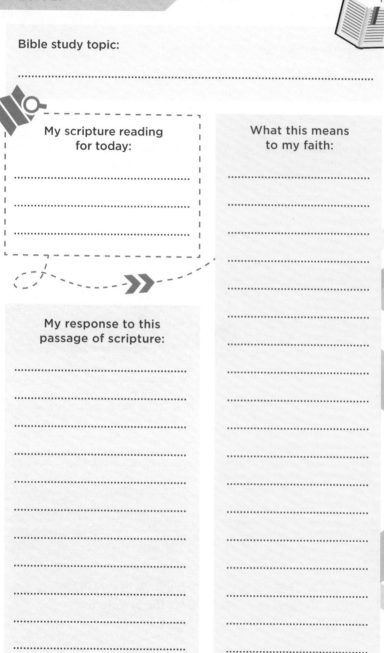

DATE:

Bible study topic:

....

My scripture reading
for today:

....
....
....

What this means
to my faith:

....
....
....
....
....
....
....
....
....
....
....
....
....
....

My response to this
passage of scripture:

....
....
....
....
....
....
....
....
....
....

How it applies to my daily life:

....

....

....

Other thoughts on this topic:

....

....

....

....

....

....

....

....

....

....

....

Questions I have for digging deeper into scripture:

....

....

....

....

....

My prayer for today:

....

....

....

....

....

....

Your love, GOD, fills the earth!
Train me to live by your counsel.
PSALM 119:64 MSG

Bible study topic:

....

My scripture reading for today:

....

....

....

What this means to my faith:

....

....

....

....

....

....

....

....

....

....

....

....

....

....

....

....

My response to this passage of scripture:

....

....

....

....

....

....

....

....

....

....

....

How it applies to my daily life:

....

....

....

Other thoughts on
this topic:

....

....

....

....

....

....

....

....

....

....

....

....

Questions I have for digging
deeper into scripture:

....

....

....

....

....

My prayer for today:

....

....

....

....

....

....

*Like newborn babies, you must crave pure spiritual
milk so that you will grow into a full experience
of salvation. Cry out for this nourishment.*
1 PETER 2:2 NLT

DATE:

Bible study topic:

....

My scripture reading
for today:

....

....

....

What this means
to my faith:

....

....

....

....

....

....

....

....

....

....

My response to this
passage of scripture:

....

....

....

....

....

....

....

....

....

....

....

....

....

....

....

How it applies to my daily life:

....

....

....

Other thoughts on this topic:

....

....

....

....

....

....

....

....

....

....

....

....

Questions I have for digging deeper into scripture:

....

....

....

....

....

My prayer for today:

....

....

....

....

....

....

I passed on to you what was most important and what had also been passed on to me. Christ died for our sins, just as the Scriptures said.

1 Corinthians 15:3 nlt

DATE:

Bible study topic:

....

My scripture reading for today:

....

....

....

What this means to my faith:

....

....

....

....

....

....

....

....

My response to this passage of scripture:

....

....

....

....

....

....

....

....

....

....

....

....

....

....

....

....

....

....

....

How it applies to my daily life:

....
....
....

Other thoughts on this topic:

....
....
....
....
....
....
....
....
....
....
....
....
....
....

Questions I have for digging deeper into scripture:

....
....
....
....
....

My prayer for today:

....
....
....
....
....
....

God, you did everything you promised, and I'm thanking you with all my heart. You pulled me from the brink of death, my feet from the cliff-edge of doom. Now I stroll at leisure with God in the sunlit fields of life.

PSALM 56:12-13 MSG

DATE:

Bible study topic:

....

My scripture reading for today:

....

....

....

My response to this passage of scripture:

....

....

....

....

....

....

....

....

....

....

....

What this means to my faith:

....

....

....

....

....

....

....

....

....

....

....

....

....

....

....

....

....

....

How it applies to my daily life:

....

....

....

Other thoughts on
this topic:

....

....

....

....

....

....

....

....

....

....

....

....

Questions I have for digging
deeper into scripture:

....

....

....

....

....

My prayer for today:

....

....

....

....

....

....

*"But if you remain in me and my words
remain in you, you may ask for anything
you want, and it will be granted!"*
JOHN 15:7 NLT

DATE:

Bible study topic:

....

My scripture reading for today:

....

....

....

What this means to my faith:

....

....

....

....

....

....

....

My response to this passage of scripture:

....

....

....

....

....

....

....

....

....

....

....

....

....

....

....

....

....

....

....

How it applies to my daily life:

....
....
....

Other thoughts on this topic:

....
....
....
....
....
....
....
....
....
....
....
....

Questions I have for digging deeper into scripture:

....
....
....
....
....

My prayer for today:

....
....
....
....
....
....

They have made God's law their own,
so they will never slip from his path.
PSALM 37:31 NLT

DATE:

Bible study topic:

....

My scripture reading for today:

....

....

....

What this means to my faith:

....

....

....

....

....

....

....

....

My response to this passage of scripture:

....

....

....

....

....

....

....

....

....

....

....

....

....

....

....

....

....

....

....

How it applies to my daily life:

....

....

....

Other thoughts on
this topic:

....

....

....

....

....

....

....

....

....

....

....

Questions I have for digging
deeper into scripture:

....

....

....

....

....

My prayer for today:

....

....

....

....

....

....

But be doers of the word, and not hearers only.
JAMES 1:22

DATE:

Bible study topic:

....

My scripture reading for today:

....

....

....

What this means to my faith:

....

....

....

....

....

....

My response to this passage of scripture:

....

....

....

....

....

....

....

....

....

....

....

....

....

....

....

....

....

....

....

....

....

....

....

How it applies to my daily life:

....

....

....

Other thoughts on this topic:

....

....

....

....

....

....

....

....

....

....

....

Questions I have for digging deeper into scripture:

....

....

....

....

My prayer for today:

....

....

....

....

....

....

*"Know this with all your heart, with everything in you,
that not one detail has failed of all the good things
GOD, your God, promised you. It has all happened.
Nothing's left undone—not so much as a word."*

JOSHUA 23:14 MSG

DATE:

Bible study topic:

....

My scripture reading
for today:

....

....

....

My response to this
passage of scripture:

....

....

....

....

....

....

....

....

....

....

....

....

What this means
to my faith:

....

....

....

....

....

....

....

....

....

....

....

....

....

....

....

....

....

How it applies to my daily life:

....

....

....

Other thoughts on this topic:

....

....

....

....

....

....

....

....

....

....

....

....

Questions I have for digging deeper into scripture:

....

....

....

....

....

My prayer for today:

....

....

....

....

....

....

Above all, you must realize that no prophecy in Scripture ever came from the prophet's own understanding, or from human initiative. No, those prophets were moved by the Holy Spirit, and they spoke from God.

2 PETER 1:20–21 NLT

DATE:

Bible study topic:

....

My scripture reading for today:

....

....

....

What this means to my faith:

....

....

....

....

....

....

....

....

....

My response to this passage of scripture:

....

....

....

....

....

....

....

....

....

....

....

....

....

....

....

....

....

....

....

How it applies to my daily life:

....

....

....

Other thoughts on this topic:

....

....

....

....

....

....

....

....

....

....

....

....

Questions I have for digging deeper into scripture:

....

....

....

....

....

My prayer for today:

....

....

....

....

....

....

GOD promises to love me all day, sing songs all through the night! My life is God's prayer.
PSALM 42:8 MSG

DATE:

Bible study topic:

....

My scripture reading
for today:

....

....

....

What this means
to my faith:

....

....

....

....

....

My response to this
passage of scripture:

....

....

....

....

....

....

....

....

....

....

....

....

....

....

....

....

....

....

....

....

How it applies to my daily life:

....

....

....

Other thoughts on this topic:

....

....

....

....

....

....

....

....

....

....

....

....

Questions I have for digging deeper into scripture:

....

....

....

....

....

My prayer for today:

....

....

....

....

....

....

Every word of God proves true. He is a shield to all who come to him for protection.

PROVERBS 30:5 NLT

DATE:

Bible study topic:

....

My scripture reading for today:

....

....

....

What this means to my faith:

....

....

....

....

....

....

....

....

....

....

....

....

....

....

....

My response to this passage of scripture:

....

....

....

....

....

....

....

....

....

....

....

How it applies to my daily life:

....

....

....

Other thoughts on this topic:

....

....

....

....

....

....

....

....

....

....

....

....

Questions I have for digging deeper into scripture:

....

....

....

....

....

My prayer for today:

....

....

....

....

....

....

But the word of God increased and multiplied.
ACTS 12:24

DATE:

Bible study topic:

....

My scripture reading for today:

....

....

....

What this means to my faith:

....

....

....

....

....

....

....

....

....

....

My response to this passage of scripture:

....

....

....

....

....

....

....

....

....

....

....

....

....

....

....

....

....

How it applies to my daily life:

....

....

....

Other thoughts on this topic:

....

....

....

....

....

....

....

....

....

....

....

....

Questions I have for digging deeper into scripture:

....

....

....

....

....

My prayer for today:

....

....

....

....

....

....

And now I commend you to God and to the word of his grace, which is able to build you up and to give you the inheritance among all those who are sanctified.

ACTS 20:32

DATE:

Bible study topic:

....

My scripture reading for today:

....

....

....

What this means to my faith:

....

....

....

....

....

....

....

....

....

....

....

....

....

....

....

....

My response to this passage of scripture:

....

....

....

....

....

....

....

....

....

....

....

How it applies to my daily life:

....

....

....

Other thoughts on this topic:

....

....

....

....

....

....

....

....

....

....

....

....

Questions I have for digging deeper into scripture:

....

....

....

....

....

My prayer for today:

....

....

....

....

....

....

The Lord looks down from heaven on the children of man, to see if there are any who understand, who seek after God.

Psalm 14:2

GREAT BIBLE STUDY TOPICS!

Don't know where to begin with your Bible study?

Check out the following topics and recommended scripture references.

Acceptance (Judging)...........Matthew 7:1, 2; Romans 15:7; Ephesians 5:21

Anger...........Psalm 37:8; Proverbs 15:1; Galatians 5:19, 20; Ephesians 4:26; 1 Timothy 2:8; James 1:19, 20

Anxiety...........Psalm 55:22; Matthew 6:25; Philippians 4:6

The Church...........Romans 12:5; Ephesians 4:4-6; 11-13; 1 Peter 4:10

Contentment...........Matthew 6:19-21; Luke 12:15; 1 Timothy 6:6, 10; Hebrews 13:5

Faith (Overcoming Doubt)...........Matthew 21:22; John 20:29; Hebrews 11:1, 6; James 1:6-7

Family...........Deuteronomy 11:19; Matthew 5:32; Ephesians 5:22, 25; 6:1; Hebrews 13:4

Fear...........Psalm 27:1; Hebrews 13:5, 6

Forgiveness...........Psalm 32:5; Proverbs 19:11; 24:17; Colossians 3:13; Mark 11:25; 1 John 1:9

Godliness (Righteousness)...........Galatians 5:22-23; Ephesians 4:22-24; 1 Peter 1:15

God's Love...........John 3:16; 1 John 4:9

Grief...........Psalm 23:1; Matthew 5:4; John 11:25-26; 16:22

Guidance............Psalm 143:10; John 16:13

Guilt............Isaiah 64:6; Jeremiah 17:9; Romans 3:10

Honesty............Psalm 15:1-3; Ephesians 4:25

Humility (Pride)............Psalm 25:9; Micah 6:8; Luke 18:14; 1 Peter 5:5, 6

Joy............Psalm 16:11; 28:7; 37:4; 97:1; Philippians 4:4; 1 Peter 1:8

Kindness (Compassion)............Matthew 25:40; Romans 12:15; Galatians 6:2; Ephesians 4:32; Colossians 3:12; Philippians 2:4

Loneliness............Psalm 25:1, 16; Matthew 28:20

Loving Others............John 13:34, 35; 15:13; Ephesians 5:1-2; 1 Peter 4:8; 1 John 3:18

Obedience............Matthew 12:50; Luke 11:28; John 14:15

Peace............Proverbs 14:30; Isaiah 26:3; John 14:27; Romans 12:18; 14:19; Philippians 4:7

Perseverance............Galatians 6:9; 2 Thessalonians 3:13; Hebrews 10:36

Prayer............Psalm 37:7; 61:1-2; Matthew 7:7-8; Luke 18:1; James 4:8

Salvation............Acts 4:12; Romans 10:9; Ephesians 2:8-9

Society............Romans 13:7; 1 Peter 2:11, 12, 17

Suffering............Matthew 11:28; John 16:33; 2 Corinthians 4:8-9; 12:9; Hebrews 4:16; 12:2, 3

Temptation............1 Corinthians 10:13; 2 Thessalonians 3:3; Hebrews 2:18

Thankfulness............Psalm 68:19; 136:1; Isaiah 63:7; Ephesians 5:20

Values...........Proverbs 4:7; Jeremiah 9:23-24; Philippians 4:8; Matthew 22:37-40

The World...........Galatians 5:24; Colossians 3:5, 8, 9; 1 John 2:15-16

Worship...........Psalm 29:2; John 4:23-24; Hebrews 13:15

THE PRAYER MAP
for the Whole Family

The Prayer Map for Men 978-1-64352-438-2
(available January 2020)

The Prayer Map for Women 978-1-68322-557-7

The Prayer Map for Girls 978-1-68322-559-1

The Prayer Map for Boys 978-1-68322-558-4

The Prayer Map for Teens 978-1-68322-556-0

*This series of purposeful prayer journals
is a fun and creative way to more
fully experience the power of prayer!*

Each inspiring journal page guides you to write out thoughts, ideas, and lists. . .which then creates a specific "map" for you to follow as you talk to God. Each map includes a spot to record the date, so you can look back on your prayers and see how God has worked in your life. *The Prayer Map* will not only encourage you to spend time talking with God about the things that matter most. . .it will also help you build a healthy spiritual habit of continual prayer for life!

Spiral Bound / $7.99